An Apple Tree
Through the Year

An Apple Tree
Through the Year

by Claudia Schnieper/photographs by Othmar Baumli

A Carolrhoda Nature Watch Book

Carolrhoda Books, Inc./Minneapolis

Thanks to Dr. Leonard B. Hertz,
Department of Horticultural Science and
Landscape Architecture, University of Minnesota

Additional photographs courtesy of: p. 9, Washington State
Apple Commission; p. 16, International Apple Institute;
pp. 36, 38, 41, Michael E. Zins.

This edition first published 1987 by Carolrhoda Books, Inc.
Original edition copyright © 1982 by Kinderbuchverlag Reich Luzern
AG, Lucerne, Switzerland, under the title DER APFELBAUM IM
JAHRESLAUF. Translated from the German by Gerd Kirchner.
Adapted by Carolrhoda Books, Inc.

This book is available in two editions:
Library binding by Carolrhoda Books, Inc.
Soft cover by First Avenue Editions
Divisions of the Lerner Publishing Group
241 First Avenue North
Minneapolis, Minnesota 55401, U.S.A

Website address: www.lernerbooks.com

LIBRARY OF CONGRESS CATALOGING-IN-PUBLICATION DATA

Schnieper, Claudia.
   An apple tree through the year.

   Translation of: Der Apfelbaum im Jahreslauf.
   Includes index.
   Summary: Follows an apple tree through the four
seasons, detailing the yearly growth cycle and examining
the ecosystem of the entire apple orchard.
   1. Apple—Juvenile literature. 2. Apple—
Development—Juvenile literature. 3. Apple—Ecology—
Juvenile literature. [1. Apple. 2. Apple—Ecology.
3. Ecology] I. Baumli, Othmar, ill. II. Title.
SB363.S3413   1987   634'.11   87-7997
ISBN 0-87614-248-X (lib. bdg.)
ISBN 0-87614-483-0 (pbk.)

Manufactured in the United States of America
6 7 8 9 10 11 – P/JR – 04 03 02 01 00 99

Apples have been grown and eaten since ancient times. There are many stories, legends, and superstitions connected with this fruit that is a common sight at today's grocery stores and markets. Even so, how an apple grows on a tree is a mystery to many people.

This book follows an apple grower's trees, and one tree in particular, through four seasons to find out how apples grow. The small tree that is pictured throughout the book grows at the edge of the apple grower's **orchard**, or group of fruit trees. This tree is just one of many varieties of apple trees that grow in orchards all over the world. Because the development of an apple from a bud to a fruit is basically the same for all apples, no matter what the farmer's growing methods, this small tree is able to represent all apple trees.

The snow is gone, but it is still winter. The apple tree will remain **dormant**, or temporarily inactive, until the sun is stronger. The **buds** that formed on the branches of the tree at the end of the previous summer would not develop properly without this period of dormancy. These tiny buds contain all of the parts that the tree will need for a whole year's growth, including leaves and flower parts. A hairy covering protects the buds throughout the winter.

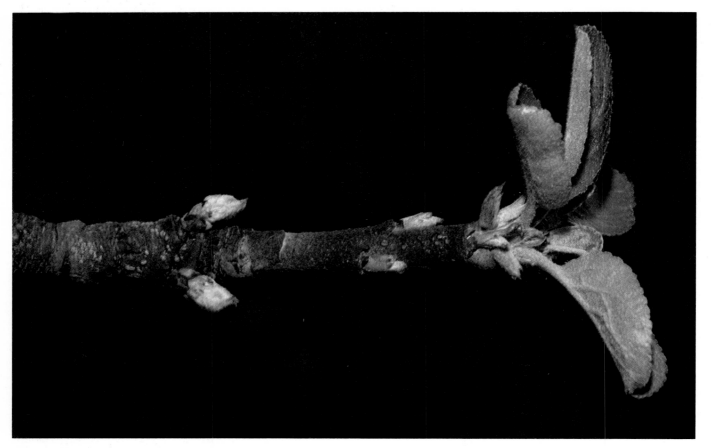

In April, when the days become warmer and longer, the leaf buds begin to open. Soon the tree is covered with green leaves, and the flower buds begin to swell. At this time, the new leaves and small flower buds covering the apple tree are especially vulnerable to destruction by **aphids** and late frosts.

Aphids are tiny insects that suck juices from plants. When they cover the young leaves of an apple tree, they can kill many of the leaves and seriously harm the tree. The ladybug is a natural **predator** of the aphid. A single ladybug

can eat up to 50 aphids a day and sometimes as many as 3,000 in its lifetime. Growers who maintain large apple orchards, though, cannot count on ladybugs to control the aphids, so they often spray their trees with an **insecticide** to kill the insects.

Without their protective coverings, the new leaves and unopened flowers are exposed to the weather and can be easily killed by a late frost. If temperatures drop below freezing, a grower may protect the trees with small stoves placed throughout the orchard.

Another way to protect the buds from a spring frost is by spraying them with water. The water protects the vulnerable buds from frost as it freezes into ice. Since water releases heat as it freezes, the grower continuously sprinkles the trees with water so that the heat necessary to protect the trees from frost is constantly generated.

In early spring, the green leaves of an apple tree are almost full grown, but the pink flowers are still closed. The **sepals**, or soft, green, leaflike flower parts, separate. As the sun gets warmer, the flowers begin to open. The flowers of apple trees range in color from dark pink to white. Most apple trees have flowers that start out pink and turn white when in full bloom.

The five sepals are still visible. Together they form a cuplike structure called a **calyx**. By the time the apple flowers have turned completely white, the dandelions are bright yellow, and most of the other trees surrounding the orchard are green. Birds are out searching for worms and insects, and bees are beginning to buzz around the apple flowers.

PARTS OF AN APPLE FLOWER

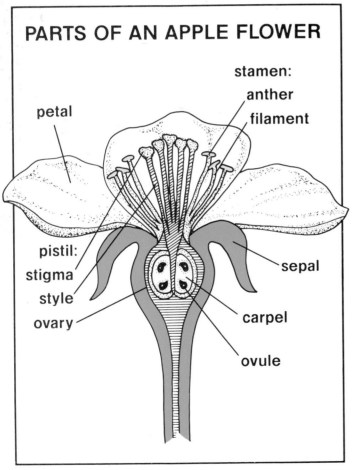

petal

stamen:
anther
filament

pistil:
stigma
style
ovary

sepal

carpel

ovule

Apple flowers have many parts. The five sepals are the first part of the flower to be seen. The sepals open to reveal the five pink **petals** of the flower. Besides these easily seen parts, there are also male and female reproductive parts in the center of the apple flower. The male parts of the flower are called **stamens** and are made up of slender **filaments** that support yellow **anthers**. The anthers produce **pollen**, a powdery yellow substance containing male reproductive cells. The stamens surround the **pistil**, or female part of the flower. The pistil is made up of five tubelike **styles**, each of which is topped by a sticky **stigma**. The pistil also includes the **ovary**, which is formed by the styles joining together at the base of the flower. Inside the ovary are five separate compartments, called **carpels**, each containing two **ovules**, or female reproductive cells that can become seeds.

In order to become seeds, the ovules must be **fertilized**. This can only happen after the apple flower is **pollinated**. Pollination is the transfer of pollen from the male part of a flower to the female part of another flower. Even though the apple flower has both male and female parts, most varieties of apple trees are not able to pollinate them-selves or other apple trees of the same variety. Apple growers, therefore, grow more than one variety of tree in their orchards. Since the trees cannot pollinate themselves, something must carry the pollen from one tree to another. Pollen can travel in the wind, but it is carried more efficiently by insects. The most reliable pollinator is the honeybee.

Honeybees are necessary for the development of apples, so apple growers encourage their presence by placing beehives at the borders of their orchards while the flowers are in full bloom. Honeybees are attracted to apple flowers by the fragrance and color of the petals and by the presence of **nectar**, the sweet liquid found in flowers. A bee that crawls around on a flower in order to get to the nectar will end up covered with pollen. When the bee flies to another tree and lands on a flower, it may brush against the pistil of the flower, leaving pollen grains

on the sticky stigma. The bee has pollinated the flower, and now fertilization
can take place.

The pollen grains that have been
transferred to the stigma send tubes
down through the styles to reach the
ovary. Through these tubes, the **sperm**,
or male reproductive cells, that are
present in pollen can travel toward and
unite with the ovules that are in the
ovary. The ovules are now fertilized
and will become seeds.

The petals, no longer needed to attract the bees, fall off, leaving the rest of the flower parts visible. Inside the ovary of the fertilized apple flower, changes that will result in the growth of an apple are taking place. If most of the ovules in the ovary have been fertilized and are growing into seeds, then the sepals will pull together, forming a sort of rounded tube. The tube looks rounded because at the **receptacle**, or base of the ovary where the flower joins the stem, the apple is beginning to swell. The sepals have closed over most of the male and female parts of the flower, but at the top of the tube the withered remains of the stamens and styles as well as the ends of the sepals can be seen. These will remain throughout the development of the apple.

The presence of the fertilized seeds makes the ovary begin to grow, and the outside part of the ovary wall produces a starchy flesh that will become the edible white part of the apple. The inside part of the ovary wall forms the core around the seeds.

Not all fertilized flowers become fruits. With two ovules in each of the five carpels, it is possible that ten seeds will grow. If only one to three seeds develop, an apple will not grow. If most, but not all, of the seeds develop, an apple will grow, but it will develop unevenly. The sides that have seeds will become rounded and fleshy and the sides without seeds will remain undeveloped.

In May or June, a tree will often lose some of its small green apples. This is a natural process that occurs because a tree can only support a certain number of apples. Many apple growers thin their trees even further, removing apples by hand or applying a chemical that makes some of the apples fall off of the tree so that the remaining apples will get more of the tree's food and energy and grow larger.

The food and energy that the tree supplies for new growth comes in the form of **glucose**, which is a sugar substance. In order to produce glucose, a tree needs sunlight, water, and a gas in the air called **carbon dioxide**.

The leaves and the roots of the tree work to gather and convert these ingredients into the food and energy the tree needs. The roots absorb water and dissolved minerals from the soil. These are carried up to the leaves through paths in the part of the tree underneath the bark.

When the water and dissolved minerals reach the leaves, the water combines with carbon dioxide, which has been gathered from the air by the leaves. With the energy supplied by sunlight, the carbon dioxide and the water mix to form glucose and **oxygen**, a gas, necessary to sustain life, that is found in our atmosphere. The oxygen is released into the air through the leaves. Water also escapes through the leaves, which is why a tree needs a constant supply of water. The tree uses the glucose to provide energy for new growth. The glucose also combines with the dissolved minerals that the tree absorbs from the soil to create tree parts such as wood, bark, and buds.

24

An apple grower helps the trees stay healthy by spraying or spreading **fertilizer** around them. The fertilizer contains some of the minerals that the tree needs to form strong branches and healthy leaves and fruit.

Apple growers have other jobs to do at this stage as well. At this time, the developing apples can easily be ruined by insect pests. One insect that creates problems for apple growers is the **codling moth**. This bark-colored moth, pictured in the top left photograph, lays its eggs on the leaves or fruit of apple trees. Out of these eggs, shown in the bottom left photograph, caterpillars soon hatch. When the caterpillars hatch, they bore holes into the apples and eat their way inside. What many people call a worm in an apple, then, is actually a caterpillar. Many apple growers spray their trees with an insecticide at the end of the summer to protect their apples against the codling moth as well as other insect pests.

As summer turns into fall, the apples ripen. Many of the animals living in the orchard become pests at this time. The dormouse, which is found in many European apple orchards, comes out at night to feed on the new apples.

The apples are almost ready to harvest now. They have continued to grow by creating more and more of the starchy material that surrounds the seeds. About two weeks before the apples are **harvested**, or picked, a layer of cells grows where the stem of the apple connects to the tree, cutting off the apple's supply of food and energy from the tree.

The apple is able to supply its own food and energy, though, by changing the starch in its fleshy insides into sugar. It is this last ripening process that makes apples sweet. This final ripening time is also when the skin of the apple (if it isn't a green-skinned variety) begins to change color. The change in color is caused by sunlight reacting with the sugar that is in the apple, creating red or yellow **pigments**, or color-producing materials.

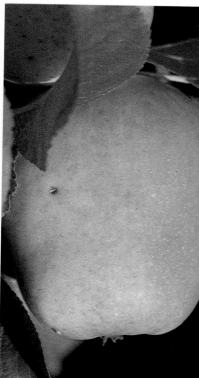

An apple may begin to change its color late in the summer, but it is not ready to be picked until the fall. Apples are harvested in the fall, usually during September and October. The biggest and best apples are picked by hand. The pickers are careful not to bruise these apples because they are to be sold as fresh fruit. Here the apple grower is picking apples from some of his larger trees.

The apples are picked and put into baskets, which are then emptied into crates. These apples will be sorted, and only the best will be sold as fresh fruit. Apples that will be used to make apple cider, applesauce, or other apple products are usually shaken down from the tree either by hand or by a mechanical shaker.

Apples that are not sold right away are stored in cool storage areas. The cool temperatures keep the fruit fresh and allow apples that are picked in the fall to last until the following summer.

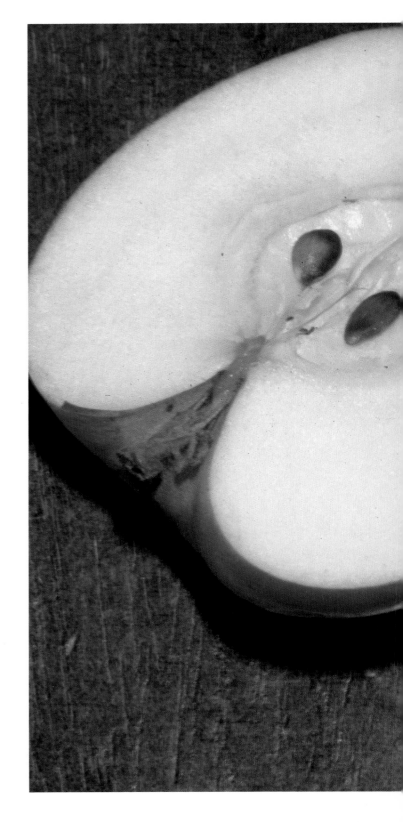

A grower does not want to store any bad apples such as the one pictured on the far right. The damage done by a codling moth caterpillar can easily be seen when such an apple is cut open. Whereas the apple to the immediate right is well formed with juicy, white flesh, the apple on the far right, which has been home to a codling moth caterpillar, is small and unfit to eat. In the good apple, you can see the seeds in the carpels.

Now that the apples are harvested, the apple tree prepares itself for winter by completing the formation of the new buds that began developing in the summer. After the tree has produced the buds, the leaves start to change color, and soon they fall. The fallen leaves decay, and nutrients that are present in the leaves enter the soil, providing food for the tree and other plants.

At this time in the orchard, creatures are preparing for winter as well. Birds pick up and eat apples that have fallen to the ground. The codling moth caterpillar burrows underneath the bark of the apple tree where it will spend the winter in a cocoon. It will emerge in the spring as a moth.

The tree prepares itself for winter, and the apple grower does some additional work on the tree in preparation for the coming year. In late fall, growers carefully **prune**, or cut, the branches of their trees to control the direction of the branches' growth. The shape of an apple tree is important. If it grows without attention, it will become bushy, and the top of the tree will shade the lower branches. The leaves on the lower branches would then be unable to gather essential energy from the sunlight.

Finally winter has come, and all of the apple trees are covered with snow. The cold period of winter is a time for the tree to rest, and the buds, protected by their hairy covering, will remain dormant until spring. In the spring, the buds will break open, and the whole cycle of apple growth will begin again.

GRAFTING

How was this orchard of trees begun? The apple trees described in this book are all **domesticated** trees, or trees whose growth is controlled by humans. Trees that grow wild from apple seeds usually produce apples that bear little resemblance to their parent apples. This is because the seed has a complicated background. An apple seed is the product of two different trees. One tree provided the ovule and the other tree provided the sperm to fertilize the ovule. The seed has characteristics of both trees. With so much cross-fertilization, an apple seed can contain characteristics of many different kinds of apples. Trees grown from seeds, therefore, produce apples with a blend of characteristics that create an apple that is different from either of its parent apples.

Apple growers know which apples grow and sell the best in the regions where they live, and they want to be sure that their trees will produce the right varieties of apples. The apple trees in commercial orchards, then, are not trees grown from seed, but are domesticated trees that are a product of a process called **grafting** that joins together parts of different trees to create a new tree.

There are a number of ways to graft. A **cleft graft,** like all grafts, joins a **rootstock**, or healthy section of tree with roots, with a **scion**, or a living section of a tree branch that supports one or more dormant buds. The scion is taken from the kind of tree the grower wants to produce. To make a cleft graft,

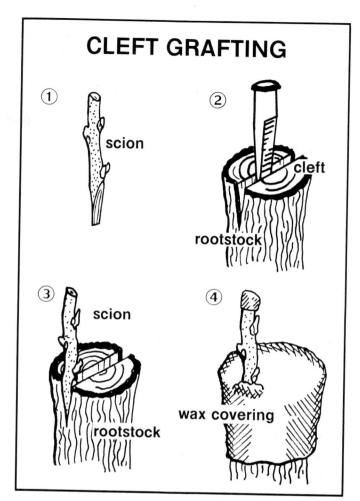

CLEFT GRAFTING

① scion

② cleft
rootstock

③ scion
rootstock

④ wax covering

a cleft, or slit, is made in the rootstock and is gently wedged open. The scion, cut to expose the parts of the branch underneath the bark, is then inserted into the cleft. The open cut is then bound up or covered with wax to protect it from the weather and from disease. The living tissues of the scion and the rootstock will soon join, creating a new tree. As this newly created tree matures, it will begin to produce only the variety of apple that was produced by the tree from which the scion was taken. Growers buying trees created by grafting, therefore, know exactly what variety of apple they are getting.

Grafting can be used to create new trees, and it is also possible to gradually change an existing wild tree to grow any variety of apple by slowly grafting new scions to the old tree. Such a tree could even be made to grow more than one kind of apple.

There are many kinds of apples, each with a slightly different color, shape, or taste. All commercially grown apples are the product of domesticated trees. The Russet, pictured in the top right photograph, is an apple that keeps well and is often used in cooking. The red apple shown in the bottom right photograph

is called an Idared because it was grown for the first time in the state of Idaho. Jonathan apples, pictured above, are juicy apples that are good for eating but do not keep very well. To the left is the widely grown Golden Delicious apple, which has a very sweet taste.

These apples were grown in different places to be used in many different ways, but each is the product of an apple tree that has been carefully tended through the year.

GLOSSARY

anther: the part of the stamen that produces and holds pollen

aphid: a very small insect that sucks the juices of plants

bud: a small, covered bulge on a tree limb or plant stem that contains parts that will develop into leaves or flowers

calyx: a cuplike structure formed by the sepals of a flower

carbon dioxide: a gas which is absorbed from the air by plant leaves

carpel: the ovule-bearing part of a flower

cleft graft: a graft which joins a rootstock and a scion by means of a cleft made in the rootstock

codling moth: a moth whose caterpillars live in apples and other fruits

domesticated: a plant or animal that has been adapted to be of some use to humans

dormant: temporarily inactive

fertilize: to unite male and female reproductive cells so that new life may develop

fertilizer: a substance, usually manure or a mixture of chemicals, used to make soil richer in nutrients

filament: the stalk of the stamen

glucose: a form of sugar that is produced by and used as a food and energy source by green plants

grafting: to join together a scion and a rootstock

harvest: to gather a crop

insecticide: an agent, often chemical, that kills insects

nectar: a sweet liquid found in plants

orchard: a group of planted fruit trees

ovary: the rounded basal area of a pistil

ovule: a female reproductive cell. When fertilized, an ovule becomes a seed.

oxygen: a gas, necessary to sustain life, that is found in our atmosphere, water, and most rocks and minerals

petal: the part of a flower that attracts insects by its color and scent

pigment: color-producing material that is present in plants and animals

pistil: the female organ in the center of a flower, made up of a stigma, a style, and an ovary

pollen: fine, yellow "dust" that is produced by the anther of a seed plant and contains sperm

pollinate: the transfer of pollen from the anther of one flower to the stigma of another

predator: an animal that kills other animals for food

prune: to cut away and shape a tree or plant for more efficient growth

receptacle: the part of a flowering plant where the flower joins the stem

rootstock: a section of tree with roots that is used as part of a graft

scion: a living section of a tree branch that supports one or more dormant buds and is used in a graft. The scion determines the kind of fruit the tree will produce.

sepal: green, leaflike structures that make up a flower's calyx

sperm: a male reproductive cell

stamen: the male reproductive part of a flower made up of an anther and a filament

stigma: the sticky top of a flower's pistil

style: the part of a pistil connecting the stigma and the ovary

INDEX

ABOUT THE AUTHOR

Claudia Schnieper is a free-lance editor, translator, and journalist. She is the author of five children's books including the Carolrhoda Nature Watch book *On the Trail of the Fox.* She lives with her husband, Robert, various cats and dogs, and a parrot in an old farmhouse near Lucerne, Switzerland.

ABOUT THE PHOTOGRAPHER

Othmar Baumli is a photographer and a commercial artist; nature photography is his main interest. His photographs illustrate several adult books and two children's books. Mr. Baumli lives with his wife and daughter in Meggen, a small village near Lucerne, Switzerland.